AN IRISH ROADSIDE CAMERA
1919-1939

AN IRISH ROADSIDE CAMERA
1919-1939

Motoring's Golden Years

Bob Montgomery

Dreoilín

For
Kate

BY THE SAME AUTHOR
An Irish Roadside Camera 1896-1906 – The Pioneering Years
Early Motoring in Ireland
Leslie Porter - Ireland's Pioneer Racing Driver
The Irish Grand Prix 1929-1931
The Phoenix Park Speed Trials 1903
The Irish Gordon Bennett Race 1903 (Dreoilín Album)
Ford Manufacture and Assembly at Cork 1919-1984
The 1903 Irish Gordon Bennett - The Race that Saved Motor Sport
Down Many a Road - The Story of Shell in Ireland 1902-2002
An Irish Roadside Camera 1907-1918 – The Years of Growth
Racing in the Park
A Lifetime's Collecting – The Legendary Car Collection of Jim Boland
Great Drives – 22 Great Irish Roads
The Royal Irish Automobile Club

Published by Dreoilín Specialist Publications Limited,
Tankardstown, Garristown, County Meath, Ireland.
Telephone: (00353) 1 8354481
e-mail: info@dreoilin.ie
Website: **www.dreoilin.ie**

Trade enquiries to Gill & Macmillan,
Telephone (00353) 1 5009500
Distribution by Gill & Macmillan

First Published in October 2011

Copyright © 2011 Bob Montgomery

ISBN 978-1-902773-23-0
A CIP record for this title is available from the British Library

Design by Dreoilín Specialist Publications Limited, set in Bembo by Alan Pepper Design and printed in the Republic of Ireland by Naas Printing Limited

CONTENTS

INTRODUCTION

The first two volumes of this series, *An Irish Roadside Camera - The Pioneering Years 1896-1906* and *The Years of Growth 1907-1918* told the story of the early years of motoring in Ireland for the first time. They did so by the use of evocative photographs drawn primarily from the Archive of The Royal Irish Automobile club, of which I am fortunate to be the Curator. Irish people, I have always felt, have a particular fascination for old photographs. Perhaps, because so much of the detail of our history has been lost, old photographs evoke a strong reaction amongst us, and properly contextulised, they can bring a tale such as this to life in a way words alone cannot do.

Many of the photographs in this selection have not been seen for at least eighty years — some for almost one hundred years and they tell a story which is part of our social history and which has, for too long, been part of a hidden history.

Once again, I have drawn heavily on the resources of the Royal Irish Automobile Club Archive and in particular many photographs that first appeared in the pages of The Motor News magazine. Sometime the quality of the photograph is not of the quality I would prefer for publication, but where it has a particular merit I have included it despite this.

The period covered by this new volume was a period of hope. The horrors of the First World War were receding and a peaceful future beckoned. Those who could afford to embraced it and its pleasures, one of the chief of which was the freedom motoring provided. Alas, peace was to be elusive but for a period just over twenty years all forms of motoring and motorsport flourished before the storm clouds gathered once more.

I hope that you, the reader, will once again enjoy this small effort on my part to reclaim a small part of our history which has been ignored far too long.

Bob Montgomery,
September 2011.

LIST OF PHOTOGRAPHS

CHRONOLOGY OF MOTORING IN IRELAND
1919 - 1939

1919   Permit Strike
        Irish Automobile Club becomes Royal Irish Automobile Club in recognition of its member's humanitarian work during
        The Great War.
        Tractor production begins at Ford in Cork.

1923   Model T production begins at Ford in Cork. Tractor production ceases.

1928   Start of RAC Tourist Trophy Races at Ards circuit. The series continues until 1936.

1929   First RIAC Irish International Grand Prix on the Phoenix Park circuit.

1931   Final RIAC Irish International Grand Prix. A race is also held in 1930.
        The first Ulster Motor Rally is organized by the UAC. The event in due course becomes The Circuit of Ireland Rally.

1932   Irish Motor Racing Club (IMRC) commences series of national and international races at Phoenix Park that continue
        until the outbreak of war in 1939.

1934   Leinster Motor Club (LMC) organises first Leinster Trophy Race at Skerries circuit.
        IMRC organize first Cuairt Bhré street race at Bray. Races are held there again in 1935.
        Ulster Automobile Club (UAC) organize first County Down Trophy race on Donaghadee circuit.

1935   Leinster Trophy race moves to new circuit at Tallaght where it continues to be held until 1939.
        UAC County Down Trophy race moves to new Bangor circuit. It is held there again in 1936.
        Ford claims more than 50% of car sales in the Irish Free State.
        The Limerick Motor Races are organized by the IMRC on a street circuit in Limerick city. They are repeated in 1936
        and 1938.

1936   IMRC organise a race on the Carrigrohane circuit on the outskirts of Cork. The race is held again in 1937.

1937   UAC runs the International Ulster Trophy race on a new circuit at Ballyclare.

1938   IMRC Cork race becomes The Cork Grand Prix, the only race ever held to current Formula 1 regulations in the Irish
        Free State.
        The 25,000 Cork-built Ford rolls off the production line.

1939   Petrol rationing begins in October in the Irish Free State.

THE OPEN ROAD IN A GOLDEN AGE

From the earliest days of pioneering motoring in Ireland (roughly 1896-1906) through the years of growth (1907-1918), and despite the relatively small number of motorists involved, progress was more swift that one might have supposed. But the real impetus to motoring in all its forms in Ireland was to result from the Great War and the return home of large numbers of able-bodied men who had over the years of the war learned to exist with the motorcar and motorcycle as an integral part of their daily lives in the armed forces.

This provided a familiarity with motorised machinery that had previously been lacking in an Ireland that had generally been bypassed by the Industrial Revolution, unlike our near neighbour across the Irish Sea. No longer would the motorcar be primarily the plaything of the well-off. Rather it would now be something that the man-in-the-street would aspire to, and if most cars were beyond his means, well then, the car manufacturers would 'cut their cloth' to suit his budget. As a result motorcycling boomed in the 1920s and a new breed of car was born, the 'Light Car'. The 'Light Car' was just what the name given to it described, a car reduced to its bare essentials and with a smaller engine, relying on its very lightness for its performance. In many ways it was a re-invention of the motorcar and could be compared to the introduction of Microlight aircraft in recent years that were essentially a re-invention of the light aircraft that had become overly complex and expensive.

At the same time as this increased wish to own some form of motorised transport so too there was a great awakening to the beauties of our island. The motor and motorcycle magazines continually ran articles exploring the lesser-known parts of Ireland while motoring guidebooks flourished as never before. Appropriately, the most popular of these guide books by far was *Mecredy's Road Book of Ireland,* which was published in two volumes – The Northern Section and the Southern Section. When first published, the motorcar did not exist and the Mecredy Road Books were written for the benefit of touring cyclists, and evolved into a guide written mainly for the benefit of motorists and motorcyclists.

One of the key pieces of information contained in the Road Books was concerning the state of the roads the touring motorist was likely to encounter. For most touring motorists this was a subject of some concern, and rightly so, for there were few good roads with a good surface and the bad roads were very bad indeed.

Driver: "Isn't this road simply awful?"
Guest: "Absolutely the worst I've ever tasted."

But as the 1920s turned into the 1930s steady progress was made and the remoter parts of Ireland became accessible to those who wished to explore by road. What awaited these adventurous motorists was an unspoiled landscape and a generous welcome. In *Mecredy's Road Book of Ireland* it was remarked that no other country, with the possible exception of Switzerland, contained such varied scenery packed into such a small space. Those who explored it in the 1920s and 1930s may not have known it but they were seeing it in a golden age of motoring.

(1) Facing page: Slea Head, County Kerry.

(2) **The Devil's Elbow in the Valley of Glencullen, on the borders of the Counties of Dublin and Wicklow, was a typical piece of road over which touring motorists traveled. Such roads, although without a tarmac surface, served motorists and motorcyclists well in Motoring's Golden Years as they set out to explore further and further afield.** *Source: The RIAC Archive*

(3) To the west of the current road from Killarney to Kenmare, the old road between the two crossed The Windy Gap at its highest point. Today the road is a cycleway and foot trail. *Source: The RIAC Archive*

(4) Looking today exactly as it did in the 1920s, the well-known ford at Glenmalure, is still a challenge for motorists at certain times of the year. The car seen here crossing it in the mid-1920s is a six-cylinder Nash. *Source: The RIAC Archive*

(5) The Automobile Association (AA) came to Ireland in the second decade of the last century and provided a much needed set of services for Irish motorists. One of their innovations was the establishment from 1927 on of a network of telephone boxes to which their members had a key. In the case of a breakdown the telephone could be used to request assistance. This AA Telephone box at Shankill was the first to be installed; the second was at Carryduff, County Down.
Source: The RIAC Archive

(6) The 'AA man' and his sidecar full of tools and emergency equipment were a familiar sight to touring motorists in the 1930s.
Source: George Stuart

(7) A feature of the Killarney to Kenmare road, both then and now, is the series of tunnels on the Kenmare side. Rough-hewn out of the rock they facilitated access to Kenmare and opened up a vast area of Kerry to touring motorists. R J Mecredy, the Editor of *The Motor News* magazine lobbied hard for them to be built and for a number of years the road was known as 'Mecredy's Road'.

Source: The RIAC Archive

(8) Sometimes the going could be pretty rough! This 12hp Swift is tackling a rough stretch of the road on Ligoniel Hill near Belfast. Touring motorists accepted such rough stretches, and the punctures that often ensued, as part of the experience of touring, the pleasures of which far outweighed such inconveniences. The four-seater Swift, incidentally, cost £685 in 1921.
Source: The RIAC Archive

(9) Historic Glendalough was a favourite destination of touring motorists in the 1920s and 30s, as indeed, it still is today. The Royal Hotel at Glendalough was often the focal point of a journey to Glendalough, as with this fine 19.6hp Crossley.
Source: The RIAC Archive

(10) Traveling further afield to Britain or the Continent involved a sea passage, and it was prohibited for vehicles to carry any more than a minimal amount of petrol in their fuel tank aboard ship. The AA was on hand at the ports to assist its members by using this special suction pump to remove the petrol from their fuel tanks.

Source: The RIAC Archive

(11) No 'roll-on, roll-off' ferries in the 1920s and 30s! Every vehicle had to be labouriously winched on and off. This special tackle was devised by the B&I Shipping Company for loading and unloading cars at Holyhead and Dublin.

Source: The RIAC Archive

(12) John Hilliard, of the Lake Hotel, Killarney, at the wheel of the 14hp Crossley that he had just put in service for the use of visitors to the Lake Hotel. Beautifully situated, The Lake Hotel today still welcomes touring motorists.
Source: The RIAC Archive

(13) A 19.6hp Crossley with the Upper Lake at Glendalough in the background. Glendalough was perhaps the most visited place by touring motorists in the 1920s and 1930s.
Source: The RIAC Archive

(14) A Nash car touring somewhere in the west of Ireland. Roads such as this were fine in the dry when dust was likely to be the main problem, but in the wet could turn into a greasy quagmire.
Source: The RIAC Archive

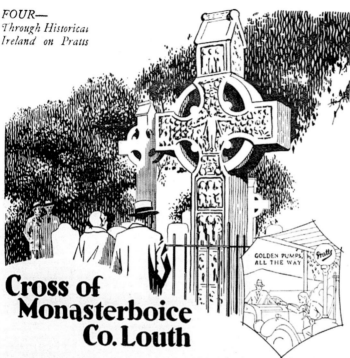

FOUR—
*Through Historical
Ireland on Pratts*

Cross of Monasterboice Co. Louth

GOLDEN PUMPS, ALL THE WAY

The Boyne Valley makes one of the most interesting trips which the motorist can take. Five miles from the mouth of the river is the historic town and port of Drogheda. A few miles up the river are the Royal cemeteries of the Irish Kings of 2,000 years ago, the most famous being New Grange. Northward are the ruins of Mellifont Abbey, founded by the Cistercians in 1142. Fourteen miles from Drogheda are the ruins of Monasterboice, an ancient walled enclosure. There is a lofty round tower, two ruined Churches and three crosses, two of which are among the grandest of the high crosses in the country. The largest is 27 feet high and over 6 feet across its arms, the whole being richly carved with religious scenes and interlaced ornaments. Further on are the Hill of Tara and Tailteann (or Teltown) where the famous games were held.

The Roads all along this interesting trip are good, many of them being first-class. Everywhere there are ample supplies of Pratts, the always reliable, always pure petrol.

Never say "petrol"—say

PRATTS

IRISH-AMERICAN OIL CO., LIMITED, 1 & 2 Upper O'Connell Street, Dublin

(15) Not surprisingly, the petrol companies were quick to encourage the development of touring by motorists. A typical example of one of the ways they did so is this advertisement by Pratts, one of a series featuring places of interest to the touring motorist, in this case, the cross of Monasterboice in County Louth.
Source: The RIAC Archive

(16) A Delage car entering the Irish Free State from Northern Ireland in 1924 at the frontier post on the main Newry to Dundalk road. Such crossing points manned by Customs officials were a feature of cross-border traffic right up into the 1980s.
Source: The RIAC Archive.

(17) An ancient ferry used to connect Tyrone and Armagh at Maghery. Touring motorists were likely to encounter such ferries throughout the entire island.
Source: The RIAC Archive

(18) Roche's Hotel in Glengarriff pictured in 1937. In the early days of motoring, hotels encouraged touring motorists by keeping stocks of petrol. By the end of the 1930s they were reaping a substantial benefit from the development of touring in Ireland as this varied car park demonstrates.
Source: George Stuart

(19) The pretty village of Adare in County Limerick has always attracted touring motorists and is today a busy tourist destination. In the 1920s one was as likely to see a flock of sheep being herded down its main street past the Dunraven Arms Hotel as one was to see another touring car.
Source: The RIAC Archive

IRISH MOTORISTS AND THEIR CARS

The road conditions encountered by Irish motorists in the 1920s and '30s were incredibly varied but on the whole, could be classed as 'poor'. In the pioneering age, one of the great menaces encountered by Irish motorists was dust. In dry weather the roads were covered in a layer of dust that made following another car at the very least very unpleasant and often almost impossible. That dust remained a problem is evidenced by the cartoon from the pages of *The Motor News* magazine in the early 1920s reproduced on page 17. Was it any wonder that this was the time when cars began to be open to the elements less often and fully enclosed areas for the driver and his passengers became much more the norm.

In the rain, the dusty surface of these roads turned into a gooey slippery mess that must have made driving a most unpleasant task. And even those roads that had a decent surface were prone to pot-holes (what's different about that, I hear you say), and punctures and suspension damage were common.

And it wasn't just the surface of the road that the driver had to contend with; on many roads there were fords to be tackled. Given the relatively primitive electrics of the time these fords could be a considerable barrier and of course, a ford was one thing to tackle when the water was not too high, but when it was in flood after sustained heavy rain then it was likely to be insurmountable.

Of course, it was not just the natural obstacles a motorist had to contend with. In the earliest days of motoring, the biggest problem was horses and their owners. Unused to cars and their noise, an encounter with a horse usually led to the horse, at the very least, rearing up, and most probably bolting. In some instances their owners were little better behaved. Early motorists grew used to having to pay out compensation on the spot to angry owners.

The Seeds of Ambition

Over time the horses, and perhaps more importantly, their handlers, grew accustomed to the passage of cars, and the problem all but disappeared. However, livestock on the roads remained a problem and sheep and hens were, it seems, the most common offenders. Herds of sheep being moved along the road remained a problem right into the 1950s but in the 1920s and 30s were a difficulty encountered by the touring motorist on a frequent basis.

But to more than offset all these natural - and unnatural - hazards, the touring motorist had the opportunity of seeing Ireland at its most beautiful and to add to that often there was the special thrill of venturing where few motorists had ventured before. Imagine the thrill of discovery experienced by these early touring motorists as they explored into the more remote parts of Kerry, Connemara or Donegal. It's hard to imagine more beautiful routes of discovery anywhere in Europe. And yet, such routes were available to touring motorists all over Ireland.

(20) Hard to imagine that the crossroads seen in the back of this 1920 photograph of JC Percy in a Rolls-Royce is today one of the busiest junctions in Ireland! JC Percy had been the editor and proprietor of *The Irish Wheelman* magazine, a rival of Mecredy's *Motor News*. In 1903, the two combined forces and *The Irish Wheelman* was wound up. Percy became an influential figure in the British and Irish motor trade over the next thirty years, during which time he also continued to write regularly for The Motor News.
Source: The RIAC Archive.

(21) Mrs Hugh McAllister and her Cluley 10hp Light Car. Messrs. Cluley of Coventry, long established bicycle manufacturers of some thirty years standing, manufactured this, their first car in 1921, although they had manufactured a tri-car, the Globe Cymocar, in 1904.

Source: The RIAC Archive

(22) An 11.4hp Humber saloon photographed outside the entrance to Leinster House, Dublin. Leinster House was then the headquarters of the Royal Dublin Society, in addition to its showgrounds at Ballsbridge.

Source: The RIAC Archive

(23) Mathis cars were first manufactured in Strasbourg from 1898 to 1903 but these early cars were all experimental prototypes and the first car they sold to the public in 1904 and 1905 was the Hermes designed by Ettore Bugatti. The first Mathis to be designed in-house didn't appear until 1910 and when the company re-established itself after World War 1 they offered sporty models with small engines, being early followers of a creed of performance through lightness, their slogan being "'Ware the enemy - Weight". This is their sports two-seater model and is pictured touring in Connemara.

Source: The RIAC Archive

(24) Motorists in the 1920s and 30s were not deterred by bad weather conditions, as this photograph taken in the Dublin Mountains shows. Considering the lack of creature comforts (most particularly a heater) and the rudimentary tyres fitted to these vehicles. In such conditions every journey must have been an adventure.

Source: The RIAC Archive

(25) The wonderfully named Moon car was a product of The Moon Motor Car Company of St. Louis in the United States. Rare in Europe, this 6-cylinder model 3.6 litre was first introduced in 1919 and amongst other feature, its radiator was a copy of that of Rolls-Royce. (Later radiators copied those of the Belgian make, Minerva). Its likely that the driver of this Moon car, a Mr. WE Fitzsimmons, was associated with the motor trade as very few Moon cars seem to have made their way to Ireland.
Source: The RIAC Archive

(26) In complete contrast to the Moon, Amilcar was one of the sporting *voiturettes* that proliferated in France after World War 1. The type shown here had a 1 litre 4-cylinder sv engine with three forward speeds. In reality, they were little different from their competition but Amilcar were by far the most successful and famous of these makes. They ceased production of cars upon the outbreak of World War 2 in 1939.
Source: The RIAC Archive

(27) Swift of Coventry started out making sewing machines, and progressed through bicycles, motor tricycles and quadricycles to cars. After World War 1 they enjoyed considerable popularity in Ireland and were immensely strong and robust even if not very powerful. This example belonged to WE Crawford, a well-known Irish rugby fullback at the time this photograph was taken in 1928. Sadly, Swift went out of business in 1931, being unable to compete with such mass-produced cars as the Austin.
Source: The RIAC Archive

(28) On an unidentified beach, but most probably Tramore in County Waterford, this touring couple and their Ford car typify touring motorists in the Golden Age of Motoring in Ireland. They took full advantage of their newfound motoring freedom and were adventurous enough to explore all over Ireland.
Source: The RIAC Archive

(29) By the 1920s the motor car had found its way into all aspects of Irish life. At the Ladies Golf Championship at Newcastle Golf Club in the early 1920s, the lady golfers competing in the championship were taken on a tour of the surrounding countryside and our picture shows the noted golfer, Major Hezlet, about to set off with his passengers in his Sunbeam car.

Source: The RIAC Archive

(30) WG Wilkinson at the wheel of his 12hp Rover car in 1920. Rover was one of the great British makes in the period between the two World Wars. Like Cluley, they had built a reputation based on their bicycles before turning to car production with a four-wheeled design in 1904.
Source: The RIAC Archive

(31) Another 11.4hp Humber – this time an open tourer - at the Glenview Hotel, in the Glen of the Downs, in Wicklow, another favourite haunt of early touring motorists.
Source: The RIAC Archive

TRADE AND COMMERCIALS

The establishment of the Free State and the financial constraints it had to navigate during the period from its founding up to the declaration of 'The Emergency' in 1939 ensured that the motor trade in Ireland had a bumpy and erratic ride through the 1920s and 30s. Many were the motor garages founded in optimism but few stayed the course and those that did generally lived on their wits to survive. The economic war and the restrictions it imposed led to the establishment of assembly operations for a surprisingly wide variety of makes of cars, including a number of American marques.

Yet very often a mere handful of these makes were assembled before the reality of selling cars in Ireland set in. Our only true indigenous manufacturer, Chambers Motors in Belfast, struggled to re-establish itself as a car manufacturer after the war and carried large unpaid debts – like so many car manufacturers who had switched to munitions or other war work during the conflict – which the British Government was slow to pay. Eventually, in 1924, it was forced to give up the unequal struggle.

Henry Ford and Son at Cork was a different situation, the vast factory at Marina having been established to be the world's largest tractor manufacturing plant. But just as it was getting into production, the war ended and demand for tractors fell away. The plant switched to other manufacture over the following years – trucks, cars, back to tractors for a time and then finally once more to cars. In fact, Ford cars were so successful in the Irish market that in the final years before 'The Emergency' they captured more than 50% of the Irish market. Cork also boasted the Dunlop Tyre factory alongside the Ford plant at Marina, and these two operations were by far the most successful motor industry businesses in Ireland in this period.

Despite all these problems, garages sprang up all over the country. Many of these owed their origins to their owner having learned mechanics skills during the First World War. Their arrival on the Irish scene coincided with the arrival of bulk storage for petrol and the introduction of kerbside petrol pumps in most villages and towns throughout the country. At the same time the major oil companies, Pratt's which would change it's name to Esso at a later date, and Shell, began to employ the forerunner of the modern petrol tanker, 600 gallon bulk tankers, that considerably simplified the delivery and storage of petrol. In addition, the petrol supplied by the major oil companies was for the first time consistent in quality, something that had been a major bone of contention for Irish motorists prior to this. Bus services spread out across the country and the many private bus companies provided a service that supplemented the train in many areas. Many of these buses were newly commissioned modern vehicles and were important in providing increased mobility for country dwellers.

Garage Proprietor: "How often have I to tell youse two gazebos to pipe down when there is a lady around? Here's Lady Dragonsblood on the phone complaining of your filthy language this morning.
What was it this time?"
Mick: "Me an' Tim had a few words, but we didn't use no langwidge. I started to scald out the radiator, not knowin' Tim was underneath and some of it went on his neck, so he yells out 'Good gracious me, mate! Please be careful!' ".

(32) The staff of Messrs. Wayte Brothers Limited, Leeson Street, Dublin, photographed in 1920. By then, the larger establishments were occupying purpose-built premises in prominent positions in the High Street.
Source: The RIAC Archive

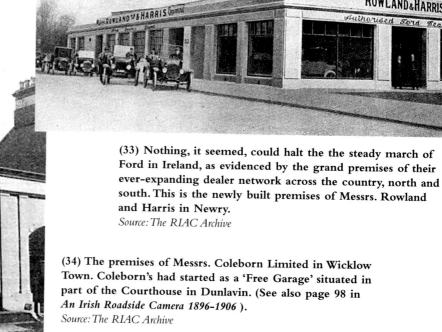

(33) Nothing, it seemed, could halt the the steady march of Ford in Ireland, as evidenced by the grand premises of their ever-expanding dealer network across the country, north and south. This is the newly built premises of Messrs. Rowland and Harris in Newry.
Source: The RIAC Archive

(34) The premises of Messrs. Coleborn Limited in Wicklow Town. Coleborn's had started as a 'Free Garage' situated in part of the Courthouse in Dunlavin. (See also page 98 in *An Irish Roadside Camera 1896-1906*).
Source: The RIAC Archive

(35) By the early 1920s, bulk tank petrol installations were becoming more common in garages, replacing the old system of two and five gallon cans. To service these new installations, the oil companies began to introduce a fleet of 600 gallon tankers, or as they were then known, 'tank wagons'. This Anglo-American Oil Company tanker, one of the first introduced, was built on a Daimler CJ type chassis.
Source: The RIAC Archive

(36) Clanwilliam House in Dublin was typical of many fine purpose-built garage premises that were built in the 1920s. Note for the first time a greater area is given over to the display of cars for sale. Bean, Berliet and Lancia commercial vehicles were distributed in the Irish Free State from this premises.
Source: The RIAC Archive

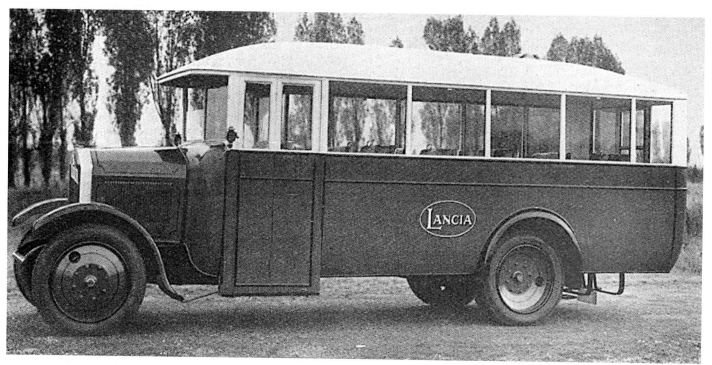

(37) This was also the period when the bus companies became established with a whole host of private operators introducing new routes to supplement the still extensive railway network. This handsome 26-seater Lancia is one of a fleet of three introduced by Clanwilliam Motors Limited, one of the many private bus operators. *Source: The RIAC Archive*

(38) In January 1938, Messrs. Henry Ford & Sons factory at Cork reached the milestone of the 25,000th car to roll off the production line since 1932, when the assembly of Ford cars and trucks commenced at the Cork plant. Ford dominated car and truck sales in the Irish Free State during the 1930s taking over 50% of the market in 1935.
Source: The RIAC Archive

(39) One of the first 'kerb-side' petrol pumps in Ireland, this Gilbert and Barker storage tank installation was installed outside the premises of the Nassau Motor Company in Nassau Street, Dublin, in February 1921.
Source: The RIAC Archive

(40) Inset: The last word in petrol dispensing in the 1920s, this type of pump also introduced the illuminated globe which was to become such an iconic feature of the garage scene over the next fifty years.
Source: The RIAC Archive

(41 & 42) Two interesting photographs from a publication by the Royal Institute of Architects in Ireland. *'A Cautionary Guide to Dublin'*, published in 1933. The publication was intended to show what was being achieved and what could be achieved with everyday buildings in Ireland. It's hard to imagine a greater contrast between the garage in the upper photograph and the thoughtfully designed garage in the second photograph.

Source: The Royal Institute of Architects in Ireland

(43) The 1920s was the era of 'The Light Car', smaller, lighter, cheaper cars reduced often to their basics they nevertheless brought affordable car ownership within the reach of a great many for whom pre-war it had been an impossible dream. GN was one of the most popular and best of the Light Car makes and this fine example was photographed outside the premises of The Irish Motor and Engineering Company Limited in Percy Place, Dublin.
Source: The RIAC Archive

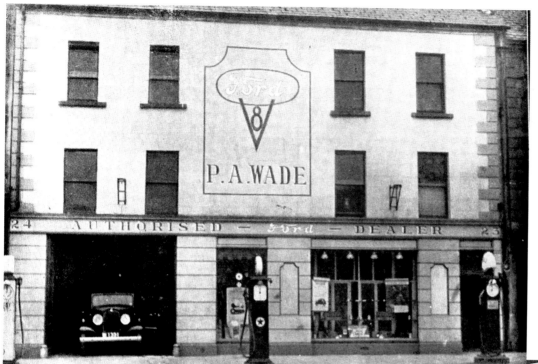

(44) PA Wade was a typical Irish Ford dealer in a county town, photographed here in the 1930s. Note the three kerbside pumps and the entrance into the garage and workshops. There is only a tiny showroom and the premises are located in the town centre.
Source: The RIAC Archive

(45) Thompson's Motor Car Company in Dublin was one of the leading garages in the city. This picture was taken on the occasion of the opening of a new entrance to their premises in Great Brunswick Street, now Pearse Street, where the majority of the motor trade was based in Dublin.
Source: The RIAC Archive

SELLING THE DREAM

The 1920s and 30s saw a flowering of advertising directed at Irish motorists. As advertising reflects the social conditions of the time, it's well worth examining examples of this advertising for what it tells us about motoring in this time.

Two of the great advertisers of the time were Shell-Mex and CC Wakefield & Company, later to become known as The Castrol Oil Company. Both companies produced striking advertising, that of Shell being some of the finest produced anywhere in the period. CC Wakefield took a different tack, concentrating on a series of advertisements that featured the endorsements given to their products by various manufacturers, an important factor at a time when product quality varied enormously from oil company to oil company. The approval of Ford of Cork or Hillman or Austin meant a great deal at the time.

Castrol also developed 'Success' advertising based on the motorsport success of various drivers and teams they supported in high-profile motorsport events. Their sponsorship of the many record-breaking cars and motorcycles of the time was a further endorsement of their products and served to reinforce the manufacturers endorsement that their products were of the finest quality and could perform in the most extreme conditions.

The manufacturers were also quick to advertise their motorsport success, an excellent example being the Sunbeam Motor Car Company of Wolverhampton who in 1923 extensively advertised their success in the *Grand Prix de France* at Tours when Henry Segrave drove a 6-cylinder Sunbeam racing car to a breakthrough victory for a British car. Another name that produced strongly individual advertising was the Irish Dunlop Company who manufactured tyres at Cork beside the Ford factory.

Much of the advertising was quite fascinating: In 1920 John Hutton & Sons of Summerhill in Dublin were advertising that they had been building coaches and carriages since 1754; the first advertisements for Hire Purchase were appearing from Bowmaker – (Hire Purchase had been around since the early days of motoring in Ireland but was something a gentleman did not speak about even if he took advantage of it as "The easiest system of car purchase") - and the Erne Motor Company of Baggot Street, Dublin, was advertising motorcycles ranging from a Raynal from £24 to an expensive Rudge at £65. 10 shillings, while a sidecar could be had for just £15.

Unsurprisingly, the manufacturers of cars were the most regular advertisers and Wolseley and Austin were two of the most frequent. Wolseley described their products as "The cars of Luxury & Economy" while Austin launched the "sensational Austin 10" as the modern height of elegance with improved road comfort and safety plus speed and economy.

Finally, mention must be made of advertising intended to convey information about the many new traffic regulations that were introduced particularly in the 1920s. This was a time when a standard set of road signs was introduced in Ireland and Britain as well as several European countries. The Irish-American oil Company through its advertising for its Pratt's petrol explained many of the new regulations, reflecting the beginnings of major changes for Irish motorists.

IN
1754
WE WERE BUILDING COACHES AND CARRIAGES.
MAY WE BUILD A MOTOR BODY FOR YOU
IN
1920
JOHN HUTTON & SONS LTD., Summerhill **DUBLIN.**

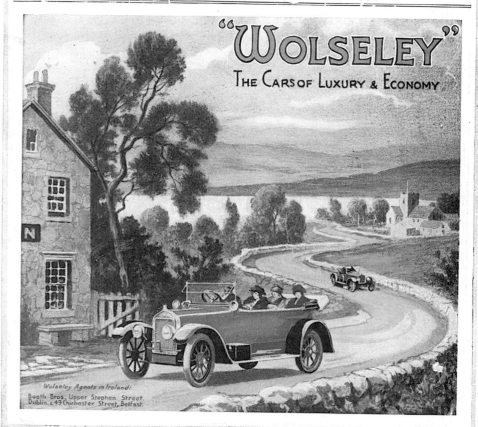

(46) *The Motor News* was founded in 1900 by the remarkable RJ Mecredy, who remained its editor until his death in 1924. The magazine would continue to be published up until the end of 1939 when supplies of paper could no longer be obtained. It was the bible of Irish motorists and the advertising space on its front cover was much sought after by the motor manufacturers for their advertising. Wolseley cars were among the most frequent advertisers on its cover during the 1920s and 30s. *Source: The RIAC Archive*

(47) Shell advertising was among the most distinctive in the 1920s and 30s. Strong images and an assurance of their petrol's quality were their main themes as well as the joys of touring and the open road.
Source: The RIAC Archive

GUARANTEE!

Every Shell Pump is examined, passed, and SEALED by a Weights and Measures Inspector, thus guaranteeing accurate measure from

SHELL

petrol

PUMPS

SHELL-MEX (DUBLIN), LIMITED
70, Grafton Street, Dublin.

Telegrams: "Shelmex, Dublin."   Telephones: Dublin 3168, 3169, 3170.

(48) With the introduction of bulk installations and petrol pumps, Shell 'guaranteed' the accuracy of their pumps – a powerful statement to motorists of the time.
Source: The RIAC Archive

Major H. O. D. Segrave in the winning Sunbeam GRAND PRIX de France

(49) Manufacturers used the motorsport success of their products to sell their everyday cars, and such successes were seen as powerful endorsements by the car buying public.
In this fairly typical example, Sunbeam are advertising the success of Major HOD Segrave in winning the French Grand Prix at Tours.
Source: The RIAC Archive

THE SUPREME
SUNBEAM

FURTHER SUCCESSES
GRAND PRIX
DE FRANCE
TOURS, JULY 2nd
2 LITRE (14 h.p. Type) 6-cyl.

On June 23rd at Fanoe, Denmark, Capt. Malcolm Campbell, driving a 12-cyl. SUNBEAM, fitted with Dunlop Cord Tyres, broke the world's speed record for one mile from flying start in 26.14 secs.
137.7 m.p.h.

On June 29th, at Porthcawl, Capt. Malcolm Campbell, driving a 6-cyl. SUNBEAM, covered the mile from standing start in 47.2/5 secs., passing the winning post at
110 m.p.h.

1912. Coupe de l'Auto France.
SUNBEAM FIRST : SECOND : THIRD.

1914. Tourist Trophy, I.O.M.
SUNBEAM FIRST.

1922. Tourist Trophy, I.O.M.
SUNBEAM FIRST.

SUNBEAM
1st 2nd & 4th

Driven respectively by

H. O. D. Segrave.   Albert Divo.   K. Lee Guinness.

THE SUNBEAM MOTOR CAR CO., LTD.
Head Office and Works - - WOLVERHAMPTON.
Manchester Showrooms - - - 106 DEANSGATE

AUTHORISED DEALERS :—T. J. Rogers, 42 South King Street. Dublin; The Lincoln Motor Co., 4 Lincoln Place, Dublin; Bailey Bros., Eyre Square, Galway; T. J. Dunne and Co., 25 Mitchel St., Clonmel; V. H. Robb and Co., Ltd. Chichester Street, Belfast.

(50) The 1920s saw for the first time the introduction of many new rules and regulations for motorists. Such seemingly simple things as standard signals from a points duty policeman were introduced and the petrol companies were instrumental in running advertising campaigns to educate the Irish motorist.
Source: The RIAC Archive

(51) Right from the earliest days of motoring, CC Wakefield and Company (Later The Castrol Oil Company) had a clear message for motorists based on the endorsement of their products by the majority of car manufacturers backed up by their sponsorship of racing and record breaking. This Irish advertisement features the endorsement of Ford, very important in a market where Ford consistently held over 50% of all car sales.
Source: The RIAC Archive

WHEN YOU BUY A FORD ... YOU BUY "Mechanical Engineering"

WHEN YOU BUY WAKEFIELD PATENT Castrol MOTOR OIL - YOU BUY "Fluid Engineering"

HENRY FORD & SON LTD. CORK OFFICIALLY APPROVE PATENT CASTROLITE IN WINTER AND PATENT CASTROL XL IN SUMMER

C. C. WAKEFIELD & CO. (IRELAND) LTD., 15 BARROW STREET, DUBLIN

(52) Another CC Wakefield advertisement for Castrol Motor Oil; this time featuring the endorsement of its products by Hillman, one of the leading makes of the time.
Source: The RIAC Archive

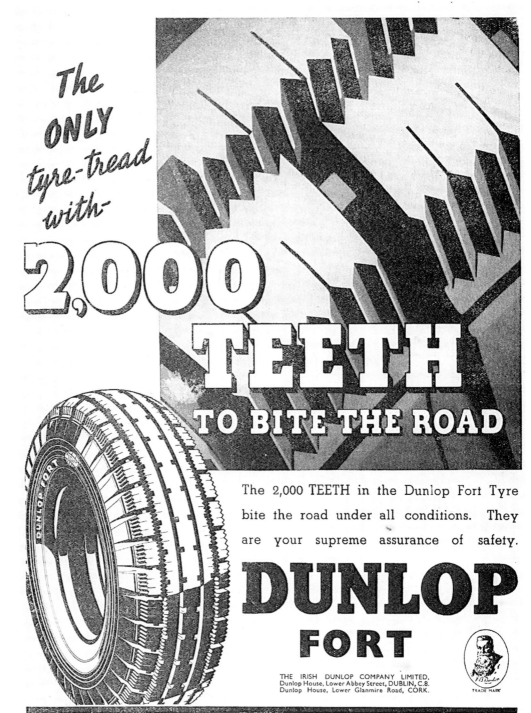

(53) The other major manufacturer of automotive products besides Ford at Cork was Dunlop. Together, these two companies were the most significant players in the Irish Motor Industry during the 1920s and 30s. During this time the majority of vehicles in Ireland were shod with Dunlop products, appropriately, as the pneumatic tyre had originated in Ireland in 1890.

Source: The RIAC Archive

AUTOBIKES
AND
MOTORCYCLES

Ride a Motor Cycle and enjoy motoring in its healthiest and most economical form. A Motor Cycle costs you less to buy and less to run—and enables you to enjoy the fresh air and countryside.

RAYNAL	£24
FRANCIS BARNETT	£25 10s.
NEW IMPERIAL	£42
MATCHLESS	£55 15s.
RUDGE	£65 10s.

Any make supplied. Sidecars from £15

Catalogues Free—State which required.

Any machine may be purchased by **EASY MONTHLY INSTALMENTS.**

Low Insurance Premiums arranged.

FREE TUITION. SERVICE AND SATIS-FACTION GUARANTEED.

ERNE MOTOR Co.,
17 Lower Baggot St., DUBLIN.
Agents everywhere—Write for terms.

(54) Motorcycles enjoyed their own Golden Age during this period and specialist sellers sprang up all over the country. This advertisement by the Erne Motor Company of Lower Baggot Street, Dublin, offered a selection of motorcycles ranging in price from the Raynal at just £24 to the highly regarded Rudge at £65. Sidecars, then enjoying their greatest popularity, could be had from just £15,
Source: The RIAC Archive

THE IRISH INTERNATIONAL GRAND PRIX

Between 1913 when the last of the Irish Automobile Clubs Reliability Trials was held and 1929 there was virtually no motorsport in the Irish Free State other than Trials and Sprints. In Northern Ireland the situation was better with the Craigantlet Hillclimb an annual fixture and in 1927 the start of the series of Tourist Trophy Races at the Ards circuit.

Enthusiasts in the south looked enviously at these events, particularly the Ards TT races and wondered why no similar events took place there. In fact, since as early 1924 the members of the Royal Irish Automobile Club had been seeking to organize a major motor racing event. Various schemes were put forward by interested parties and it was only natural to invite the foremost Irish drivers of the day – Kenelm Lee Guinness and Major Henry OD Segrave – to inspect the proposed course in Dublin's Phoenix Park. With the success of the Ards TT races in 1927, the RIAC redoubled its efforts to bring motor racing to the Phoenix Park. There were many difficulties to be overcome, not the least of them financial, and a Guarantee Fund was established with the intention of holding an international race in July 1929. There was great support from the motor trade as well as other interested groups with the result that the fund was eventually oversubscribed.

There was also a physical problem with the proposed Phoenix Park circuit. Right in the middle of what would be the main straight on the proposed course sat the Phoenix monument. For the Speed Trials held in the park in 1903 the sides of the monu-

ment had been removed to allow the competing cars in the speed trials to pass by in safety, but now it needed to be removed altogether if the proposed race was to be held. However, with the enthusiastic support of the government of the Irish Free State the statue was moved to a new site outside the Vice Regal Lodge.

In January 1929 an official announcement that the race would go ahead was made, although curiously, no decision had yet been taken as to whether the course would be clockwise or anti-clockwise. This was decided by Kenelm Lee Guinness in favour of a clockwise circuit in February 1929 when he inspected the proposed course.

Meanwhile, the RIAC had decided that the event would be titled The Irish International Grand Prix and would be run over a circuit some 4 miles and 460 yards in length. Incredibly, there was some criticism of the length of the course as being too short as it was felt that the faster cars would have to overtake the slower cars too often for safety during the course of the proposed seventy laps. Partly to counter this, the RIAC decided that the race should be run over two days on a handicap basis with a race for the smaller engined cars on the Friday (The Saorstát Cup) and the race for the larger engined cars (over 1,500cc) on the Saturday (The Éireann Cup). The winner of the Irish International Grand Prix would be the driver who completed the course in the shortest possible time in either race. Thus was set the scene for three magnificent Grand Prix meetings.

(55) The Le Mans style start of the 1929 Éireann Cup race. Tom Thistlethwaite's white supercharged Mercedes is in the foreground beside the Bentley of Captain HRS Birkin. He would set an average of 82 mph over the early laps before being forced to retire with gasket problems on the 27th lap.
Source: The RIAC Archive

(57) Kenelm Lee and Algernon Guiness, along with their friend, Major Henry Segrave, gave considerable assistance and advice to the organizers of the Irish International Grand Prix. Here, Kenelm Lee Guinness addresses the drivers and their mechanics prior to the start of Friday's race in 1929.
Source: The RIAC Archive

(56) Bryan de Grineau at work sketching the most exciting incidents from the Grand Prix. The two major British motor magazines, *The Motor* and *The Autocar* both employed outstanding artists to record the most interesting incidents in races, it being quicker to reproduce their drawings than to use photographs that took longer to process and prepare for printing. Bryan de Grineau, along with Gordon Crosby, were the outstanding artists doing such work.
The RIAC Archive

(58) The Lea-Francis team lined up outside the premises of ST Robinson in South King Street, Dublin, prior to the 1929 event. Jimmy Shaw, one of the team members, was the first Irish driver home in the opening Saorstát Cup race. ST Robinson was for many years the chief scrutineer of the RIAC. *Source: The RIAC Archive*

(60) Henry Birkin 'Tiger Tim' presses on during his gritty drive in his Alfa Romeo during the 1931 Éireann Cup race of which he was the winner at an average speed of 83.80 mph.
Source: The RIAC Archive

(61) On the right is WH Freeman, of the Dublin & District Motor Cycle Club and Chief Marshal at the Grand Prix with 'Ebby' Ebblewhite, the official timekeeper at Brooklands.
Source: The RIAC Archive

Previous two pages:

(59) Tom Thistlethwaite and Henry Birkin fought an intense duel for the first 27 laps of the Éireann Cup race in 1929 before the Mercedes was retired with head gasket failure. Some idea of the vast crowd (and the lack of safety measures) can be gained from this magnificent photograph of the duel at its height.
Source: The RIAC Archive

(62) The popular satirical magazine, *Dublin Opinion*, ran special motor race issues for all three Grand Prix.
Source: The RIAC Archive

(63) The Italian racing driver, Guiseppi Campari, makes his way to his Alfa Romeo, prior to the start of the 1931 Éireann Cup Race. The somewhat larger than life Italian, a noted amateur opera singer, was injured in the eye by a flying stone in the race, but, after treatment in a nearby hospital, resumed the race on his return to the circuit.
Source: The RIAC Archive

(64) Tim Birkin and the Hon. Dorothy Paget during the 1929 event. Dorothy Paget sponsored Birkin's development of super-charged Bentleys as well as a number of aviation record-break-ing flights.
Source: The RIAC Archive

(65) A happy, informal photograph of a youthful Rudolf Caracciola during a break in practice at the 1930 event. Looking in from the right is George Mangan, who would later make a name for himself in Irish motor sport.
Source: The RIAC Archive

(66) Rudolf Caracciola and his wife 'Charly', who tragically died shortly afterwards in an avalanche. Women were not allowed in the Pit area and Charly pointedly appeared in men's clothing on the first day of practice. The ban on women in the Pit area was quietly removed by the time of the next Grand Prix in 1931.
Source: The RIAC Archive

(69) Walter Sexton was the person most responsible for the success of the Irish International Grand Prix races. Irish motorsport's most prestigious award, the Sexton Trophy, is named in his honour.
Source: The RIAC Archive

(67) President WT Cosgrave meets Boris Ivanowski prior to the start of racing at the 1929 Irish International Grand Prix.
Source: The RIAC Archive

(68) Cariccola is congratulated by President WT Cosgrave after his fine win in the 1930 Éireann Cup Race win.
Source: The RIAC Archive

(70) GVB Cooke photographed in 1930 with the 'Irene' Cup presented by Captain ACK Waite for the best performance by an Irish driver. Captain Waite was married to Irene Austin, the daughter of Sir Herbert Austin, for whom the cup was named.
Source: The RIAC Archive

Following the 1931 Irish International Grand Prix, a Fianna Fail government led by Eamon De Valera came into power in the Irish Free State. Minister Sean T O'Kelly confirmed the worst fears of the organisers of the Grand Prix when he announced that the government would no longer support "a rich men's pastime" withdrawing the subsidy that had made the three Irish Grand Prix possible.

The Royal Irish Automobile Club was therefore faced with no alternative but to bring the series of Grand Prix to an end, as it could not afford to bear the loss it would have incurred. This was a body blow to Irish motor sport that was just beginning to develop a racing scene directly as a result of the impetus the three Grand Prix had given it. For a while it seemed that this would be the end of racing in the Phoenix Park, but as so often happens in moments of crisis, the answer was found from within.

Prior to the running of the first Irish Grand Prix in 1929, the intention of the RIAC had been to precede the international races with a national race for Irish drivers and their cars. This had proved to be impossible to arrange for a variety of reasons but the idea had not gone away and was now revived for the 1932 races. It was decided to run two fifty-mile handicap races on a September date (17th) with the first being for cars up to 1100cc and the second for cars over 1100cc. In addition, the programme would include three races for motorcycles. The RIAC entrusted the running of the new event to the recently formed Irish Motor Racing Club (IMRC) and were supported by Lord Wakefield of Hythe who generously donated a fifty-guinea trophy to be presented to the winner of

either race who beat his handicap by the greatest margin. A huge crowd, estimated to be as many as 80,000, turned out in magnificent sunshine to witness Alan Potterton from Athboy win the under 1100cc race while in the race for bigger engined cars Ivan Waller from Derby took a fine win and the Wakefield Trophy in his Alvis at an average speed of 77.87 mph.

Adjudged to be a great success, plans were made for longer races in 1933 – the only criticism of the 1932 races being that they were too short. A new date was awarded to the IMRC in August for an international event but this proved impossible to organize owing to the worsening economic conditions in Ireland. A new date was allocated and the race meeting went ahead featuring two 100-mile races. Once again, Alan Potterton won the race for 1100cc cars, the race being notable as the Park debut of Ulsterman Bobby Baird in a Riley. Frank O'Boyle won the over 1100cc race, his efforts also gaining for him the Wakefield Trophy.

With the IMRC Phoenix Park race meeting now firmly established, the annual event went from strength to strength over the years up to the outbreak of the Second World War in 1939. The race meetings were particularly well supported by visiting British drivers amongst whom were such names as Raymond Mays, 'B Bira', Chris Staniland, Arthur Dobson, Reggie Tongue and Anthony Powys-Lybbe. For Irish drivers the Phoenix Park motor races were to provide the crucible where the sport took hold amongst Irish competitors and provided the bedrock of Irish motor racing for many years to come.

(71) The 2,876cc Talbot of O'Shaughnessy gets away ahead of P Donnelly (1,089cc Riley), and LR Briggs (847cc MG) in the 1935 Phoenix Park event. Note 'Shaughnessy's cloth cap. *Source: The RIAC Archive*

(72) **MJ Hynes is congratulated by George Statham after winning the Senior Motor Race in the 1934 Phoenix Park meeting at an average speed of 81.2 mph. The Statham Special, based on a Ford V8 was a regular front-runner in the major Irish road races throughout the 1930s.**
Source: The RIAC Archive

(73) 'B Bira' gets away first at the start of the 1937 Handicap race. The race was won by Dubliner David Yule while Bira had the consolation of fastest lap at 107.28 mph.

Source: The RIAC Archive

(74) 'B Bira', a member of the Siamese royal family, was one of the most exciting drivers of the 1930s and raced in Ireland at Phoenix Park, Ards, Cork and Limerick, on all of which circuits he was successful driving his Maserati and ERA cars. He is pictured here in the 1938 race driving his Maserati, bearing the 'White Mouse' symbol of White Mouse Racing, the team run on his behalf by his cousin, Prince Chula.
Source: The RIAC Archive

(75) The Silver Star of the Irish Motor Racing Club awarded to 'B Bira' for the first 100 mph lap of the Phoenix Park in 1936. The 100 mph made the Phoenix Park circuit the fastest road circuit in Europe.
Source: The RIAC Archive

(76) David Yule and his CMY Special, pictured here in the Phoenix Park paddock, were one of the most successful Irish car and driver combinations of the period.
Source: The RIAC Archive

(77) Raymond Mays photographed in his 1,488cc ERA just prior to the 1937 Scratch Race.
Source: The RIAC Archive

(78) The famous bandleader, Billy Cotton, was a regular competitor in the Phoenix Park and is pictured here with his wife and sons during scrutiny at Garda Headquarters in Phoenix Park prior to the 1936 event.
Source: The RIAC Archive

(79 & 80) Two pictures from the 1938 100 Mile Scratch Race which featured 'B Bira's' blue Maserati and the fabulous Multi-Union of Chris Staniland on the front row. At half distance it looked as if Bira would take his first Phoenix Park win but the engine of the Maserati failed and it was Staniland who went on to take the victory at an average speed of 97.45 mph.

Source: The RIAC Archive

(81) The final Phoenix Park meeting was held a few days after the outbreak of World War 2 in 1939. Here, Bradley leads Miss Stanley-Turner's MG round Gough Corner.
Source: The RIAC Archive

(82) More close work in the final pre-war Phoenix Park meeting as Woods (Morgan) leads Le Fanu (L.E.R.A.) round Mountjoy Corner.
Source: The RIAC Archive

THE ROAD RACING BOOM

The Ards Tourist Trophy races had first been held as early as 1928 and had pointed the way for the sport to develop but it was not until 1934 that Irish motor racing seems to have embraced the joys of road racing. In that year the first Leinster Trophy race was held on the Skerries circuit; the first County Down Trophy race took place on the Donaghadee circuit and the initial 'Round the House' street race was held at Bray.

The 13²/₃ mile Ards circuit through a mainly rural district on the outskirts of Belfast had for its first running in 1928 attracted what was claimed to be the largest ever crowd at an outdoor event held in Ireland. Some estimates put the numbers present as high as 500,000 though this seems unlikely. What is certain, however, is that through the night steamers brought visitors from the English and Scottish ports, many of them specially chartered for the occasion, while a vast assembly spent the night before the race under canvas around the circuit. And right from its first race, the series of Ards TT races attracted the cream of British drivers to tackle the challenging circuit that wound its way through the streets of Newtownards and Comber as well as the surrounding countryside.

The success of the Ards race led directly to the three Irish International Grand Prix organized by the RIAC, and then, when those races had passed into history, to other road circuits in the Irish Free State, the first of which was at Skerries, and of course, to the races that continued in the Phoenix Park until recent times.

The race at Skerries was organized by the Leinster Motor Club (LMC) and was the first race for the Leinster Trophy, Irish motorsport's oldest trophy still being competed for today. Indeed, the Leinster Trophy was to number amongst its winners, future world champions Ayrton Senna and Mika Hakkinen. The race at

Native: "That was a close shave, Mister."
Visiting Driver (new to Cork mountain foliage): "Well, it's a d__n long time since there was one around here."

Skerries proved popular with spectators and was sensationally won by a woman driver, the remarkable Fay Taylour. The Skerries circuit itself proved less popular with drivers and officialdom and was only used on this one occasion for cars, motorcycle racing becoming the norm there.

The Leinster Trophy moved to a new circuit at Tallaght in 1935 and stayed there until 1939, resuming for a single year there after the war in 1948. Meanwhile, the IMRC had been invited by the Bray town commissioner to organise a street race and the first of two races there was held in 1934. The 'Cuairt Bhre' "Round the Houses" races proved very popular and provided exciting racing but the road surface along Strand Road deteriorated in a dangerous manner made worse by a harsh winter in 1935. Sadly, the road authorities did not have sufficient resources to make the road improvements necessary for a return of racing and so the series came to an untimely end.

IMRC switched their attention to organizing a street race in the city of Limerick – races being organized there in 1935, 1936 and 1938. Again, these were both very popular with the public and the drivers and the three events run there were amongst the most important held on any Irish street circuit. This was true 'street racing', the entire circuit being within the confines of the city streets.

Finally, came the Cork motor races organized from 1936 to 1938 over a very fast circuit incorporating the long Carrigrohane Straight. Interestingly, the 1938 Cork Grand Prix was the only race ever held in the Irish Free State organized to the then current Formula One regulations. This landmark race was won by René Dreyfus driving a Delahaye during that marque's brief flowering.

(83) Divo driving hard in his Bugatti through Conway Square in Newtownards during the 1929 Tourist Trophy race on the Ards circuit. The series of Tourist Trophy races at Ards started in 1928 and continued until 1936 when an accident took the lives of eight spectators and fifteen others injured when local driver, Jack Chambers, lost control at the Railway Bridge coming into Newtownards. The tragedy caused the authorities not to allow further races on the circuit.
Source: The RIAC Archive

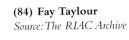

(84) Fay Taylour
Source: The RIAC Archive

(85) The first race for the Leinster Trophy was held on the Skerries circuit, the only time it was used for cars rather than motorcycles. The race was won by Fay Taylour driving an Adler, who thus became the first holder of the trophy that would include World Champion Ayrton Senna and Mika Hakkinen amongst its future winners.
Source: The RIAC Archive

(86) Sean Lemass – who would later become Taoiseach) flags away EM Mitchell (number 7) driving Redmond Gallagher's 3,622cc Urney Racing Special, RBS Le Fanu (number 17) 1,497cc L.E.R.A. and B Mason (number 33) 2,120cc Delage at the start of the 1937 Leinster Trophy race at Tallaght. The Tallaght circuit was in use from 1935 to 1939 and again in 1948.

Source: The RIAC Archive

(87) Jack Toohey, winner of the 1935 and 1936 Leinster Trophy races on the Tallaght circuit in his 933cc Smithfield Ford Special.

Source: The RIAC Archive

(88) MJ Hynes in the Statham Ford Special leads
the Bugatti of Charlie Manders and the Sunbeam of
second place WT McCalla in the 1935 Bray event.
Source: The RIAC Archive

(89) In the 1934 Bray
race, HD Walsh (MG No
18) takes Duncairn corner
closely followed by JF
Sutherland (Singer No 5).
Source: The RIAC Archive

(90) The start of the 1938 Limerick Grand Prix. The Limerick races were held in 1935, 1936 and 1938 and were amongst the best held anywhere in Ireland at this time. Excellent entries were received and most of the top British drivers of the day took part in them. The 1936 race was marred by the death of The Duke of Grafton who crashed his Bugatti fatally.
Source: The RIAC Archive

(91) The 1938 Limerick Grand Prix featured a hectic battle between the SS100 of Harold Bradley and Ernie Robb driving an MG. Neither were destined to finish as Robb's race ended on lap 7 when his engine disintegrated. Bradley continued unabated but eventually crashed into a wall, bursting both front tyres but escaping injury.
Source: The RIAC Archive

(92) 'B Bira' was the racing name used by a member of the Siamese royal family, Prince Birabongse Bhanudej Bhanubandh. Bira enjoyed a privileged lifestyle sponsored by his cousin Prince Chula Chakrabongse. He had a natural talent as a racing driver and was always popular with the crowd. He raced on all the major Irish circuits where he enjoyed considerable success driving his famous ERA racing cars, Romulus, Remus and Hanuman, as well as his Maserati.
Source: The RIAC Archive

(93) René Dreyfus driving the 4.5 litre Delahaye at Victoria House Corner during the 1938 Cork Grand Prix. Dreyfus would take victory in the race on the testing Carrigrohane circuit on the outskirts of Cork city.
Source: The RIAC Archive

94) Before the start of the 1938 Cork Grand prix, winner René Dreyfus (on right) is seen in conversation with Bira and Franco Comotti.
Source: The RIAC Archive

(95) The long straight that was a feature of the Carrigrohane circuit is clearly seen in this photograph of the pit area taken during practice for the 1938 Cork Grand Prix.
Source: The RIAC Archive

(96) The Maseratis' of Hanson and Wakefield battle it out in the 1938 Cork Light Car Race. Wakefield later went off the road at Poulavane dropping 30 feet into a field below, and wrecking his Maserati.
Source: The RIAC Archive

HILLCLIMBS, SPRINTS AND TRIALS

If motor racing had struggled to take hold in Ireland, the same could not be said of other forms of motorsport such as Hillclimbs, Sprints and Trials.

The origins of trials had been laid down in the years beginning in 1906 when the forerunner of the RIAC, the Irish Automobile Club (IAC), had run a series of highly successful Reliability Trials. These events held in 1906, 1907, 1908, 1909 and again in 1913, had vied with the Scottish Reliability Trials for being the most important event of their time and manufacturers placed great importance on success in them as a means of advertising the capabilities of their products.

In 1927 the Ulster Automobile Sports Club (later to become the UAC) made a proposal to the Motor Cycle Union of Ireland that cars should be allowed compete in a separate class in the highly successful End-to-End Trial for the Muratti Trophy. This was agreed and in that year's event two car classes – cars up to 1500cc and cars over 1500cc, were included. The 1928 event again had two car classes but in 1929 and 1930 the cars ran in a stand-alone event. However, in 1931 it was proposed that the UASC should run a motor rally over a distance of 500 miles within Northern Ireland. The proposal was agreed and the town of Bangor became the starting point of the first Ulster Motor Rally. The first winner of the event was Belfast man Jimmy McCaherty driving a 16hp Austin who managed to complete the 500 mile route without dropping a single point. By 1936 the event had changed its name to the 'Circuit of Ireland Trial' and now encompassed a route of 1,100 miles and an overnight stop in Killarney while still starting from Bangor. The event continued to grow in stature until 1939 when the Second World War brought proceedings to a stop for a number of years.

ULSTER AUTOMOBILE CLUB
OFFICIAL PROGRAMME

CIRCUIT OF IRELAND TRIAL

Starting at BELFAST & DUBLIN
Finishing at BELFAST.
APRIL 16TH - 19TH 1938

EIGHTH
ULSTER
MOTOR
RALLY

PRICE
6D.

Meanwhile, trials – both day and night – were run all over the country and proved very successful as a means for ordinary motors sport enthusiasts to compete at a modest cost. A feature of these and other events in Ireland at this time was the comradeship that existed between competitors on cars and motorcycles. So much so, in fact, that a tradition grew up of the motorcyclists providing the bulk of officials and marshals to run the car events and *vice versa*, something that was, as far as I can ascertain, unique to Ireland.

Wicklow is a natural playground for motor sport and provided many locations for hillclimbs in the 1930s, and Ballinascorney (1938/9), De Shelby (1925 and 1933 twice), Mount Venus 1932/3 and Kilternan (1935-39) were the main venues in Wicklow, while Craigantlet, first used in 1925, was the most important of the northern venues. In addition, several venues hosted Sprint events, with Turvey near Donabate (1937-39) in North Dublin, along with Deansgrange (1925) and Killeagh (Cork 1925) being the most important.

Finally, mention should be made of the often ignored sand races held at Portmarnock (1925 & 1930/31), Magilligan 1926 & 1927), Duncannon (1929-31 & 1933), Tramore (1929-33) and Duncannon 1929-31 & 1933).

(97) The start of something big! The first winner of the Ulster Motor Rally in 1931 was Belfast man Jimmy McCaherty driving an Austin 16hp Saloon. On his way to victory McCaherty completed the five hundred mile route without losing a single point. Within a few short years the Ulster Motor Rally would develop into The Circuit of Ireland Rally.
Source: The RIAC Archive

(98) A fine photograph of an Irish built 995 cc Adler Einsitzer taking part in the Donabate Sprint at Turvey. Adler cars were familiar sights at pre-war Irish racing events, entered by *'Irischer Adler Rennstall'* (Irish Adler Racing Stable).
Source: The RIAC Archive

(99) An annual event in the early 1920s was the twenty-four hours reliability trial of the Dublin and District Motor Cycle Club that was run for both motorcycles and cars over a course to Donegal and back. Our photograph shows WT Malcolmson, a very successful competitor in these trials, setting out from the starting point of the 1923 event in his G.N.
Source: The RIAC Archive

(100) Wilford J Fitzsimmons – 'Wilf' to several generations of Irish motorsport competitors – leans on the bonnet of his beloved Bugatti Brescia at the Mt. Venus Hillclimb. Wilf would twice be the winner of the Hewison Trophy before becoming a very successful Competitions Manager of the Royal Irish Automobile Club. A rock of good sense, he did much to bring northern and southern motorsport competitors together and was a founding member of the RIAC Archive.

Source: The RIAC Archive

(101) The UASC ran two twenty-five mile handicap events on the wide sands of Magilligan in June 1928, one for standard cars and one for standard sports cars. Our first picture shows GC Strachan's 1087cc Amilcar, which was second in the class for standard sports cars.
Source: *The RIAC Archive*

(102) A 1.945cc Star car, driven by WH Connolly, that did the fastest time of the day and placed third overall in the class for standard sports cars.
Source: *The RIAC Archive*

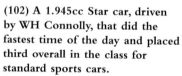

(103) W Noble's saloon-bodied Morris Cowley rounding one end of the course. It was the winner of the standard touring car class at Magilligan.
Source: *The RIAC Archive*

MOTORCYCLES AND MOTORCYCLISTS

If the 1920s and 1930s were the golden age of motoring in Ireland, it was especially so for motorcycles and motorcyclists. There was a greater than ever interest in motorcycles due to two key factors: the number of people who had been introduced to them during the recent World War 1 and also in the period post war, their relative affordability.

The result was a huge rise in the number of motorcycles on Irish roads and a corresponding increase in motorcycle sport. In fact, motorcyclists led the way in touring in Ireland and also in the development of motorsport here. And later, as interest in car motorsport developed, many of the leading exponents were drivers who had come from the ranks of motorcycle sport.

But, it was motorcycle touring that had the biggest impact. Because of their versatility, motorcycles were ideal for exploring the most remote roads on this island and the ready availability of sidecars helped make it all possible with a degree of comfort. Even today, just as in the 1920s and 1930s, it is the motorcyclists who know the most remote and best roads in Ireland, something I have discovered again and again.

As for motorcycle sport, this was a wonderful period producing many Irish riders capable of performing on a world stage. The cream of Irish racing motorcyclists belonged to this period and the foundations were laid for another generation of riders who would come to the fore in the 1950s. They cut their teeth on the various road races that came into being on tracks all over the country and on the sand races held at such venues as Portmarnock and Magilligan, and today, undeservedly somewhat forgotten.

Amongst the greatest of Irish riders was Stanley Woods who was born in 1903, and became famous for his 29 motorcycle Grand Prix wins and for winning the Isle of Man TT races 10 times during his career. He first raced in 1921 on a Harley Davidson.

Angela. "Oh, Herbert, don't the petrol fumes smell *much* sweeter in the country?"

He was so well regarded in the history of the Isle of Man TT that in 1968 a panel of experts named him as the greatest of all the island's competitors. His record of 10 wins would stand until a later era when Mike Hailwood won 14 TT races. (The record number of TT wins would also be held by another Irish rider, the late Joey Dunlop, with 26 wins).

Manliffe Barrington was another Irish rider who was successful in the TT races, although his greatest success came after the Second World War. He first competed on the Isle of Man in 1935 finishing 11th in the Senior TT Race and was another who also competed in cars finishing 4th in the Phoenix Park in 1937 driving a Rapier.

Another driver who enjoyed success on two wheels and four was Charlie Manders who was 250 cc Motorcycle champion in the late 1920's. He was a very successful private entry racing driver and drove cars such as a Delage, Sunbeams, MGs as well as Adlers, setting up the successful *'Irischer Adler Rennstall'* (Irish Adler Racing Stable).

(104) As well as Magilligan, Portmarnock Strand was a popular venue for motorsport events, in particular, motorcycle racing. Charlie Manders and Tom Byrne, were two of the biggest names in sand racing at Portmarnock. Charlie Manders was also to carve out a name for himself in motor racing events particularly driving Adler cars.
Source: The RIAC Archive

(105) The inimitable Stanley Woods was the leading Irish motorcyclist of the 1920s and 1930s achieving considerable fame at home and abroad. In this early event, Stanley is shown at the finish of the 1922 Banbridge 50 road race on his 1,000cc V-Twin Harley Davidson.
Source: The RIAC Archive

(106) A motorcycle sidecar combination pictured at 'The Red Arch' on the Antrim Coast Road. Motorcyclists led the explosion of interest in touring in Ireland.
Source: The RIAC Archive

(107) Women were very well represented for the time in motorcycle events. This is Miss Sadie Lee riding a Diamond motorcycle at the start of the Ulster Motor Cycle Club's Reliability Trial in 1925. Miss Lee went on to take the sidecar award in the event.
Source: The RIAC Archive

(108) Run in 1924 and 1925, the Hillclimb of the Drogheda Club at Knagg's Head on the Ballyboghill to Naul road was a popular event for day-trippers from Dublin. The fastest time of the day was set by CW Taylor who achieved a speed of 77.59 mph. Curiously, the spelling of the venue has evolved into 'Nag's Head' today. The photograph shows H Tate (490cc Norton) at the start of his run.
Source: The RIAC Archive

(109) The broad sands of Magilligan Strand beside the Foyle were a popular location for both car and motorcycle speed events. This is the 1925 Hundred Miles Championship that was held in wet conditions. J Craig leads eventual winner JW Shaw.
Source: The RIAC Archive

(110) JS Wright about to start his record attempt on his streamlined J.A.P. powered motorcycle on the Carrigrohane Straight on the outskirts of Cork in 1930. His speed was just over 150 mph, the fastest a motorcycle had traveled anywhere.
Source: The RIAC Archive

IRISH SUCCESS ABROAD

Irish Success abroad in the 1920s and 30s really comes down to a quartet of brave and skillful drivers: the Guinness brothers, Algernon ('Algy') and Kenelm Lee ('Bill"); Henry Segrave and the remarkable Hugh Hamilton.

Hugh Hamilton's first race was the 1930 Double-12 at Brooklands when he drove a Riley. But then, working as a salesman with University Motors, the London MG Distributors, he began an association with MGs, racing a C-type MG in 1931 and 1932 during which time he won the 850cc class of the German Grand Prix at the Nurburgring in 1932. In 1933 he was part of the successful K3 MG team at the Mille Miglia before changing to the new J4 MG in which he had what was to become a legendary duel with Nuvolari in the Ards TT - a race he should have won but for a bungled final pit stop. At the end of that 1933 season he raced the J4 in the Masaryk Grand Prix at Brno, but during a typical 'giant-killing' drive overturned and was badly injured. The following year he joined Whitney Straight's Maserati team and results came thick and fast. But at the Swiss Grand Prix on the Bremgarten circuit at Berne while driving the Maserati in the Grand Prix and while holding sixth place ahead of Fagioli and Caracciola he went off the road in terrible conditions and hit a tree. A post mortem suggested that he had suffered a heart attack, robbing Irish motor racing of one of its brightest stars.

The Guinness brothers, Algernon and Kenelm Lee, were members of the famous brewing family. Algernon first came to fame with the 200hp V8 Darracq that had been built in 1905 for the purpose of setting records. In July 1908 Algernon achieved a timed 117 mph over the flying kilometer at Oostend in it. Algernon wetted his younger brother's appetite for speed by taking him along on several of the runs on the Darracq. 'Bill' made his racing debut at Amiens in the 1913 French Grand Prix driving a 'works' Sunbeam. A burst tyre sent Bill and his mechanic into a stream from which they were lucky to emerge unhurt. His first great win came in the 1914 Tourist Trophy race on the Isle of Man, incidentally, the first great international race win by an Irishman. Bill took his racing more seriously that his brother, Algernon, and also took the World Land Speed Record at Brooklands in 1922 at an average speed of 133.75 mph. His final race was the Spanish Grand Prix of 1924, in which he crashed through a wall, plunging 50 feet down into a railway cutting. His mechanic Barrett was killed instantly and Bill received terrible injuries from which he never fully recovered.

Cuthbert: "I have always wanted to live the gay, free, careless life of a professional motor racing driver, such as I have seen on the cinema." Professional Motor Racing Driver (sadly): "So have I."

Sir Henry O'Neal de Hane Segrave was born in Baltimore but grew up on the family estate at Belle Isle on Lough Derg. He began motor racing after World War 1, first racing an Opel and then becoming a driver for the Sunbeam Company. The highlight of his racing career came in 1923 when he became the first British driver to win a Grand Prix – the French Grand Prix - a win that he followed up with other successes on the Continent in 1924, 1925 and 1926. He then set a LSR record of 203.9 mph in the Giant Sunbeam at Daytona before returning in 1929 with 'Golden Arrow' to set the LSR mark at 231.362 mph. Thereafter, he concentrated on the World Water Speed Record dying in 1930 during an attempt on the record on Lake Windermere.

(111) Hugh Hamilton was the most exciting Irish driver of the 1930s. Pictured here in the 1933 Mannin Beg race on the Isle of Man, his motor racing career was sadly short-lived but earned him a place amongst the 'greats' of Irish motorsport.
Source: The RIAC Archive

(112) **After the famous 1933 race, Hugh Hamilton is pictured with his mother, his pit manager Colonel 'Goldie' Gardner and his unnamed riding mechanic. A scheduled refueling stop mid-way in the race led to a five minute delay and his furious pursuit of Nuvolari.**

Source: The RIAC Archive

103

(113) Hamilton's pursuit of Nuvolari was made driving this 746cc supercharged J4 MG Midget. Nuvolari had never driven a K3 MG Magnette before he arrived in Belfast for the race. Eddie Hall drove the car, a works 'hack', in the Craigantlet Hillclimb the week before the TT race.
Source: The RIAC Archive

(114) Omagh born Hugh Hamilton, photographed at the Grand Prix du Penya Rhin at Barcelona in 1934. By then, Hamilton was a member of Whitney Straight's Grand Prix team and the car in the background is Whitney Straight's Maserati 8CM.
Source: The RIAC Archive

(115) Kenelm Lee Guinness in the 350hp V12 Sunbeam in which he established the last Land Speed Record to be set on a track. This was at Brooklands and was a two-way speed of 133.75 mph (215.18 kph) over the flying kilometer.
Source: The RIAC Archive

(117) The first car to travel over 200 mph, the 1927 Sunbeam driven by Henry Segrave heralded in an era of specials powered by enormous engines in an effort to take the Land Speed Record. Segrave also took the record in 1929 at 231 mph.
Source: The RIAC Archive

(116) Sir Algernon Lee Guinness was the older of the two Guinness brothers. Most notably, he drove the fearsome 200hp V8 22,518cc Darracq at a speed of 115 mph (185.7 kph) at Brooklands in 1907. He won a very wet Tourist Trophy race on the Isle of Man circuit in 1922 averaging 53.3 mph (85.78 kph) in a 16-valve Talbot Darracq ahead of team-mate Divo.
Source: The RIAC Archive

107

(118) **Fast friends – Kenelm Lee Guinness and Henry Segrave.**
Source: The RIAC Archive

(119) **The Sunbeam team photographed prior to the 1922 Grand Prix at Strasbourg. An interesting aside is the turn-out of the team cars. Chassagne's car on the left is dirty, Kenelm Lee Guinness's car in the centre is better but Segrave's, having been repainted at its driver's expense, is gleaming!** *Source: The RIAC Archive*

(120) Segrave taking the first victory by a British car in the 1923 French Grand Prix at Tours. It would be another thirty years before a British car took a win in the Grand Prix again. For this victory and his Land Speed Record achievements, Segrave became the first driver to receive a knighthood for motoring achievement.
Source: The RIAC Archive

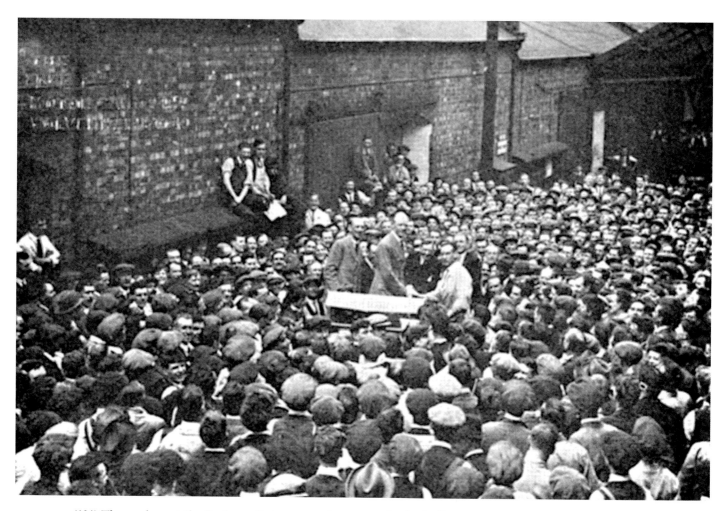

(121) The workers at the Sunbeam factory turned out to enthusiastically welcome Segrave home after his landmark victory in the French Grand Prix at Tours.
Source: The RIAC Archive

'THE OLD CROCKS'

Today, there is tremendous interest in Ireland in old cars but such was not always the case. In the early days of motoring, the pace of development was very fast and almost yearly cars were rendered outdated by the latest development. Those that could afford to purchased the latest model, and generally kept their older car, often gathering dust in outhouses. In the 1910s a large number of these older cars found a new lease of life by being converted to commercial vehicle while some were converted for use on farms as stationary motors for powering farm machinery.

Undoubtedly, this made large inroads into the population of early cars and inevitably, many were scrapped as they came to the end of their useful working commercial life or on the farm. But others survived, gathering dust in barns and outhouses where they stayed until the late 1930s. In many cases the catalyst for their rediscovery and re-birth was the series of events that the far-seeing Leinster Motor Club ran in the years 1938 to 1940.

The Leinster Run brought out a fine selection of these early cars and can be directly credited with starting the old car movement and attracted large crowds to marvel at the early cars and their crews who got into the spirit of the whole thing by dressing in costume appropriate to the age of their cars.

The first Leinster Run, soon renamed 'The Old Crocks Race' by participants and spectators alike, started from the tram depot at Donnybrook and proceeded via Dundrum, Ticknock Cross,

Stepaside, Kilternan, The Scalp, Enniskerry, Kilcroney, Bray, Shankhill, Loughlinstown and Deans Grange to the finish at St. Michael's Wharf, Dun Laoghaire.

In that first event no less than 43 cars were entered, although no record exists of how many actually started on the day. They ranged from the oldest car, a 1901 MMC driven by ARW Montgomery from Bray, to the youngest, a 1914 De Don entered and driven by T Stewart of Dublin.

Salesman: "According to our yearly depreciation chart, on a trade-in you will owe us £185 plus the price of a new car".

The first event was a great success and the event was repeated again in 1939 in front of even larger crowds, for this was an event that caught the imagination of the Irish public. So popular with spectators did the 1939 event prove that the old cars had difficulty making their way through the crowds on several sections of the route. This time there were 45 cars entered, the oldest being an 1899 Argyll driven by RD Cox from Dublin.

In September 1939, the war clouds broke and petrol rationing in the Irish Free State officially started in October . However, against all expectations, the Leinster Motor Club contrived to run the event again in 1940. Quite where the 31 entrants managed to get the petrol required is a mystery but it seems that all things are possible if people want to do them enough. This time the oldest starter was the 1900 Arrol-Johnston driven by D O'Cleary and G Wardell from Straffan. From such beginnings was the old car movement we know today born.

(122,123 & 124) The 1939 Leinster Motor Club's Veteran Run attracted very large crowds along the route as clearly seen from these three photographs. The car in the middle photograph is the De Dion that was to become so well known in the hands of the late Ossie Bennett.

Source: The RIAC Archive

(125) AH Wilkinson's rare 1905 Riley tri-car photographed on the Antrim Coast Road at the Red Arch.
Source: The RIAC Archive

(126) In the first of the Leinster Motor Club's Veteran Runs in 1938, this is the 1905 De Dion of WD McNally from Dublin, apparently enjoying the experience immensely.
Source: The RIAC Archive

(127) The 1912 Cadillac of PJ McCoole gets the attention of onlookers during the 1939 Leinster Motor club Run.
Source: The RIAC Archive

(128) An irresistible photograph of the 'Eaton schoolboys and St. Trinian's belle' – the occupants of PJ McCoole's Cadillac in the 1939 Leinster Motor Club Run.
Source: Patrick McCoole

TAIL-PIECE

(129) One of us has got to give way! Driving in Ireland has probably always had a few hazards unique to the country, and recalcient donkeys were just one of them in the 1920s and 30s.

INDEX

THE ROYAL IRISH AUTOMOBILE CLUB
ARCHIVE

The RIAC Guinness Segrave Library and Archive was established by Wilford J Fitzsimmons in 1985 with the generous support of the 3rd Earl of Iveagh. The Library commemorates two members of the Guinness family, Sir Algernon and his brother Kenelm Lee, who together with their contemporary, Sir Henry Segrave, were amongst the first Irish drivers to carve out an international reputation for themselves in the exacting world of motor sport.

The Library contains many rare volumes including 'runs' of Mecredy's *Irish Cyclist* and *Motor News.* That other early Irish journal, *The Irish Wheelman,* is also well represented within the Library, which also contains 'runs' of the more usual journals of record, *The Autocar, The Motor, Motor Sport, Speed* and of more recent times, *Autosport.* As such, the RIAC Guinness Segrave Library is an important collection of motoring literature, while its material relating to early Irish motoring is quite unique, and because Ireland took centre stage in the world of motorsport at the time of the 1903 Gordon Bennett Race, the Irish International Grand Prix series from 1929-1931 and during the golden age of the Tourist Trophy series from 1928-1936, its value as an important motoring archive is greatly enhanced.

Since 1985 the Library has continued to grow through further gifts of motoring literature and its collection of photographs, programmes and other motoring memorabilia has reached the stage where this now forms an important archive in itself. The Library is not open to the public but access is given to bone-fide researchers through the RIAC's Archive Curator. It is hoped to develop further the Dreoilín series of Transport Albums, in association with the Archive, to extend over a wide range of transport related subjects of Irish interest.

The Archive Group also includes the popular Double 20 Club for competitors who held a competition licence forty or more years ago.

If you would like to assist the Archive's work of preserving Ireland's unique motoring heritage, why not join the 'Friends of the Archive Group' – details from:

The Curator, RIAC Archive, 34 Dawson Street, Dublin 2.